## My Dog's A Democrat

Return to
Laura Shulah
5209 - 45th ST

THANK You

# My Dog's A Democrat

by Curt Brummett
illustrated by Gerald L. Holmes

DOUBLE DIAMOND BOOKS

Distributed by

**Laffing Cow Press**
PO Box 3106
Cheyenne, WY 82003
(800) 722-6932

ISBN 1-879894-01-7 paper

Reprinted 1991

## Dedication

To my Grandkids:

Joe, my calf roper; Lonesome, my general all around trouble-maker; Justa, my quiet one; and J. C. (pronounced "Ha Say"), the new kid on the block.

All these stories appeared first and in different form in *Livestock Weekly*, between January and November of 1985. Several of them also appeared in *Horse and Rider*.

This page is for John, my friend

I'll make this short and sweet. I met this man awhile back, and I told him how much I thought of his writing, and that I wished I could have the success with my material that he has had with *Hank the Cowdog*.

He told me that the only thing that would keep me from it would be to quit writing. The man gave my ego such a high I didn't come down for a week. Since the meeting in Lubbock, John Erickson has done more for my writing and story-telling than I can ever tell. The finest words I can think of could not tell how much I appreciate what he has done for me. If it weren't for him, my first book wouldn't have been the success it has been, and I know for a fact I wouldn't be getting my second book out this quick.

So here it is on paper. I appreciate everything he has done and I value his friendship. And it pleases me beyond my wildest dreams that in the writing world, thanks to John Erickson, I have the most over-paid **EDITOR** in the writing business.

Thanks John!

# Contents

## Chapter One
# Good Groceries and Clean Dishes

Used to be when I hired out to a ranch, there was one thing that I considered above all else: the food situation. Since I was single, I usually tried for a camp job with another cowboy, who could cook. I could cook, but there were several million others who could cook so much better than I could.

There is a general rule in ranching: ranch cooks are good cooks. However, I recall a time when that rule was not only broken, but so badly mutilated that the person who broke it came very close to becoming an endangered species. What I mean to say is that the cowboss put a very unfeeling person in charge of cooking.

I had hired out to a ranch in Eastern New Mexico, to help gather the renegades that had escaped roundup. The cowboss sent me to a camp and told me that the man I would be working with was a good cowboy, and as long as I made a hand, everything would be okay. He also mentioned that my new pardner didn't really like to talk a lot.

Come to find out, that was an understatement.

I got to the camp about three that afternoon, and Carlton was just turning his horse loose. I introduced myself, and he showed me around the pens, and explained about my half of the chores.

As I settled my gear in the house, he informed me that he would do the cooking and I would do the dishes. I figured since he had been there longer than me, and I didn't really like to cook that much, he had made a very good decision. I told 'im that was just fine with me.

Then he said, "The first one to gripe gets to cook and do dishes."

Now, I should have suspected something in that statement, but me being the dumb kid I was, I just ignored it. That was one mistake that I remembered from then on.

My first meal was by far the best for several days to come. It consisted of reheated stew and cornbread. And I might add that I did a splendid job on the dishes.

The next morning started a strange new dining experience that has yet to be equaled.

This man had found nineteen ways to mess up a bowl of corn flakes and I soon found out that he had his own personal style of massacre that he could use on a can of tomatoes.

One evening I mentioned that the potatoes weren't quite done, and he informed me they were scrambled eggs, and if I didn't like them I could start doing the cooking **and** the dishes.

Me being the bullheaded person I am, I smiled and said, "That's just the way I like 'em."

After about a week of eating beans that rattled like bullets when they hit the plate, and bacon that either slid off the plate and squealed as it went out the door, or shattered into a million pieces when you touched it with a fork, I was pert' near ready to start cooking, but not quite.

Then one morning after breakfast, I made up my mind that something had to be done about the way that idiot was fixing my meals.

2

I mean, when a man hands you a plate of bacon, eggs, biscuits and gravy, and the only thing you can recognize is the plate, it's time to do something.

But I kept quiet, chipped myself out a cup of coffee, and tried to eat.

It has been said that a hungry man will eat pert' near anything, but this is not always true. I know, because I was dadblamed sure hungry, and I left a bunch of whatever that stuff was on my plate.

Now folks, I'm here to tell ya it's extremely difficult to eat eggs that cackle when you cut 'em, and I have yet to figure out how he burned just half of each piece of bacon and left the other half raw. Them biscuits was so gooey, you could have used 'em for caulking compound, and they had enough salt in 'em to weigh about two pounds apiece. The gravy wasn't all that bad. I just cut it up into little bite-sized squares and put 'em in my pocket. I figured I could chew on 'em while I was riding pastures.

When I had finished my dishes and started to go catch my horse, Old Carlton mentioned the fact that I didn't eat much breakfast.

Since I had just finished washing and stacking all them dishes, I didn't throw anything at 'im. I just kinda smiled and told 'im that all those good groceries was starting to put weight on me and I had just made up my mind to start watching my waist line.

He just smiled and said any time I wanted to do the cooking, I could sure have it. But since he enjoyed it so much, he sure hoped I wouldn't take it away from him. The man was pushing his luck.

As we rode out that morning, my mind was working in high gear. I just couldn't figure this man out. I had been working with Carlton for eight days and I still didn't know his last name, and unless it was a have-to case, there was little or no conversation. And there was no way I

3

could figure out why he so cheerfully destroyed good groceries.

When we got in that afternoon, there was a hand there from headquarters with Carlton's mail and some supplies. As I helped unload the pickup, Carlton grained the horses and finished his outside chores.

The cowboy from headquarters told me how lucky I was to get on this particular camp, mainly because all the single guys wanted to work with Carlton just for the good food. Yep, it seemed like I was living with the best cook west of the Mississippi.

I thought to myself, "If the food here is considered that great, them poor boys down at headquarters must be going through pure hell." Then he told me the rest of the story.

It seemed that Carlton grew up in this area, and was a pretty good cowboy, but he always wanted to be a chef. No one really took 'im serious about his wish to cook, because he was always pulling little jokes and forever messing with someone's mind. So when he quit his job and went to cooking school, everyone figured he was just hunting new range.

After a lot of hard work and a lot of classes, Carlton finally managed to get a job in New Orleans at a big fine restaurant.

After about six years, he got the job as the head hash-slinger, and after about 12 years as the head chef, he just got tired of his job and came back home to cowboy. He hadn't changed very much. He had just gained a little weight and gotten ten times worse about messing with people's minds.

**I HAD BEEN HAD!!**

The hand from headquarters went on back and left Carlton and me to work out our differences, and by supper that night I had a plan.

4

After a meal of fried stuff, that couldn't be recognized even after the black was chipped away, I set my plan into action.

I washed the dishes pretty much the same as always, with the exception of how I rinsed 'em. I used a little extra soap, and when I rinsed the dishes off, I used cold water on half of the utensils and half of the plates. And when I stacked 'em on the shelf, I stacked 'em so's I wouldn't get the ones with the soap still on 'em.

I suffered through breakfast, lunch, supper and breakfast again. Each time the meal was worse, and each time there was just a tad more soap left on half the dishes.

After breakfast the second day, we rode out to do our rat killing. We split up to see what we could find, and figured to meet at the branding pens, and from there we would see what we could gather on our way back to camp.

I made it to the pens about one-thirty, and noticed that Carlton was already there. As I rode up I saw him take his pants off of the top rail of the corral and start putting them on.

When I got to the pens, I noticed that Carlton was kinda upset. His eyes were sunk back in his head, and he was walking like he might be a little saddle sore.

When I stepped off to get a drink and roll myself a smoke, Carlton eased over to me and said, "Pard, we need to have us a talk."

I got a drink of water, rolled myself a smoke, leaned back against the windmill tower, and said, "So talk."

Carlton worked his way around so that he was standing in the sun, so his Levi's could dry some more, took a deep breath, and started talking.

"Ya know kid, I don't want you to take this the wrong way or anything like that, 'cause I think you're doing one of the finest jobs of washing dishes I ever seen

5

in my life. But I got to thinking, just this morning, that I may be sluffing off on my cooking duties just a mite. Now, I might just be able to come up with a few decent meals every now and then if you could just see your way clear to get just a touch more soap off of them dishes.

"I haven't had the scours this bad since me and my cousin drank all that home brew, and ate that half-bushel of wild plums. I ain't been able to ride more than a quarter of a mile without having to stop and tend to business, and as you can see I was a tad slow in getting off my horse to tend to my last business, and I had to wash out my Levi's here at the windmill.

"Now since we've had this little talk, let's get on back to camp."

Well, from that time on, I ate some of the best groceries ever, and Carlton even started talking. And when I quit and went looking for newer range, I had a tactic to use on the next cook.

## Chapter Two
# Feedlot Roping with Old Bill

Very few people that have cowboyed have ever stopped to think about how easy it is for an ambitious young man such as myself to get into trouble while working.

I mean to tell ya, no matter how hard I tried to do right, there were several times it looked like I was sure doing wrong.

And I just as well tell you right now, I thought I was being singled out just because I liked to rope.

Everyone I have ever known who has worked around cattle knows for a fact that cattle have to be taught what to do. They're like little kids, and wives. If you don't get 'em trained properly early in their lives, they can develop some pretty nasty habits.

Well, I have on occasion taken it upon myself to train a cow or two. The problem with training cows, is that the process usually involves the use of a rope. And I might add, when the rope is used there is generally some overweight, slightly balding, ill-natured boss of some kind around just waiting to accuse you of roping for fun.

Very few bosses could understand why the rope was such an important tool in the proper training of a cow brute, mainly because most of the bosses I've known couldn't even spell rope, much less use one.

And 95% of the bosses who really got mad at me were feedlot bosses. That in itself should say I'm basically innocent.

Now, the few times that I have gotten into trouble in a feedyard I didn't think I should have. 'Course, that's just one man's opinion. But I'll let you be the judge.

There are two things in my life I have very rarely done. The first is that I have never been one to mouth off about anything, no matter how much I want to. I have always been the quiet type. And second, I have never pulled a rope down unless it was an absolute have-to case. And I feel pretty sure that everyone who knew me back when I was younger will tell you the same thing.

And those who try to tell you different are not remembering me, they probably have me confused with some rope-crazy idiot. And the ones who remember that are probably the bosses.

Before you start to make any rash judgement concerning my ability to get into trouble, let me explain "absolute have-to case".

Everyone knows that cow critters need to be taught respect for people who are ahorseback. And most people know that just talking to cow critters don't get it. Now, cows are creatures of habit, and like some people they can get a bad habit. And unlike some people, you can't just explain to 'em that what they're doing is unacceptable.

You have to get their attention the first time and make it count. If you don't, the cow critter will continue to use this habit to cause your life to be a little aggravating. The same can be said for wives, but this is about the proper care and training of cattle, not the care and training of wives.

The best example of a cow critter's bad habit that I can give is "bunk-crawling". Most cattle can be broken from this form of aggravation if you drive them down a feed alley, put them into a trail alley, and then drive them back to their pen.

But, some cows seem to think this is a start on a new habit, designed just to drive a cowboy crazy, and after you've driven them back to their pen a couple of times, it becomes just that.

Pretty soon, as quick as they are put through the gate in their home pen, all they do is get a quick drink of water and wait for the cowboy to get out of sight, and they go crawl right back out again.

Some of the worse bunk crawlers I've ever seen had this down to a science. They would see a cowboy coming, trot down to the gate at the feed alley, wait for the cowboy to open it, then trot to the gate going into their home pen. After being let into the pen, they would get a drink and then go visiting again.

What this means to me is that this particular cow needs to be educated. You see, the cow thinks that all a man ahorseback has to do is just take care of him personally. And I resent that kind of attitude, especially when it comes from a cow.

So here is a classic example of an "absolute have-to" case of pulling a rope down and using it to educate an elusive bovine beast in its semi-natural habitat.

I am a firm believer in the saying, "If you rope it, choke it, and 'frap' it on the ground, then turn it loose in its home pen and it will see that home is a pretty safe place to be."

I have been forced to educate hundreds of these cow critters, just to keep them from developing any more bad habits. And even though I didn't enjoy it, I felt that it was my duty as an official representative of the cowboy world, to try and do my part in keeping the elusive bovine beast (in its semi-natural habitat) from developing any really bad habits.

Of course taking on this kind of extra worry has its drawbacks. There are some people in the feedyard business who throw screamin', wall-eyed, lung-bustin' fits when they see a cowboy educating a cow critter.

Most bosses in a feed yard know that every now and then a cow critter has to be roped, but their idea of a have-to case and mine have never really matched up all that much.

I was working for a feed yard in Eastern New Mexico, and the manager was kinda silly about ropes. He seemed to think that ropes were to be used for tying gates shut and things like that.

Yep, the man was pro-cow, and anti-cowboy. He had caught me with my rope on a cow critter more than once, and more than once I had managed to get out of the situation, just barely with my job, not to mention my life.

In fact the last time he caught me educating a beef prospect, the conversation was very one-sided.

It went something like this: "The next time I see you with your rope on anything but your rope string, I'll not only fire you but I'll deduct the cost of the calf from your last pay check."

Well, that kinda got my attention. The getting fired part didn't bother me as much as having to pay for a calf, and not having any pasture to put 'im on.

Well, a couple of days after this discussion, we found a steer with a bad case of foot rot. My pen-riding pardner, Bill, seemed to think we needed to treat this case with special care, and try and get things cleared up as fast as we could. He had been going to school down at Alpine and had learned some new kind of treatment for this type of problem, and he wanted to try it out.

So we put the steer in the chute at the hospital and tried to do some work on his foot. (Fat chance.) This hospital chute was purchased at the sale Julius Caesar had when he closed out his cattle feeding operation just east of Rome, when the market cratered the first time. And I

12

might add that through the years it had been patched so many times that neither side would let down so we could get to the steer's foot.

Well, that meant just one thing.

In order for us to administer Bill's super-duper highly calculated cure-all, we were gonna have to heel this steer and lay 'im down, just to doctor his foot.

Bill really liked to rope, but he hadn't had much of a chance because of the new manager, and he had seen me get chewed out, so he just kinda let the old rope alone.

I really liked old Bill, and since he didn't get to rope all that much, I told 'im to go ahead and rope that steer, and I would tail 'im down and hold 'im while Bill doctored 'im.

Just 'cause Bill went to Alpine didn't mean he was a complete idiot. He said, "You just want me to do the roping in case we get caught. I heard what the boss said, and I can't afford to lose my job."

I assured old Bill that no matter what happened, I would explain why we had the steer down in the first place. And besides all that, we wouldn't get caught no way. The boss was in town and we wouldn't be all that long just doctoring one foot.

"Don't worry about it, I'm the one he hates to see with a rope down, and besides all that, he likes you."

Well, Bill got his horse and I turned the steer out into the trail alley and got a gate on 'im and let Bill in to do his thing with the rope.

Bill got 'im doubled on the first loop and brought 'im to me. As I reached for the tail, I noticed a slight movement at the gate coming into the hospital alley.

It was a big white Ford car, and it looked like there was steam coming from the windows.

At a second glance I noticed it was the manager's car. I looked at old Bill and said, "Boy, are you in trouble now!"

He liked to have had a cat fit, but I assured 'im I was just joking with 'im and I would explain why we had the steer down.

Well, as the manager walked into the alley, he bellered out, "Was this just absolutely necessary? And if it's not, you don't even want to hear what I've got to say."

Old Bill was totally pale, and even his horse was

kinda nervous about the old cuddly thing that had just walked into the alley.

But I stayed calm and proceeded to handle everything. And even to this day, I don't know why I said what I did.

I just looked at our fearless leader, and said, "Well sir, I didn't think we needed to rope this poor old sick thing, but Bill seemed to think this was the only way to go." I was kinda proud of myself for my quick thinking. I even kept a straight face when I said it.

There was a minor eruption of cussing from behind me and I turned just in time to duck a rock. Seemed like Bill didn't appreciate my explanation. (The boy had very little humor.)

It took quite a while to get both of 'em feeling a little better, and after we convinced the boss that we actually needed to lay that steer down, things got pert' near back to normal. The boss let us go on and doctor the steer like we started, and he left for the office. Bill wouldn't hardly talk to me the rest of the day, and it was a couple of days before he had much to say at all.

We did get a new chute for the hospital, and old Bill finally got to where he would say a few things. But when I would pull a rope down, I noticed he would disappear.

It didn't bother me though. After all, it takes a special kind of person to want to educate cattle.

## Chapter Three
# The Great American Feedyard Footrace Fiasco

One fine spring afternoon, at a feedyard in Southeastern New Mexico, we were all sitting around the scale house, taking a break from the branding shed. I was sitting there with my feet propped up, drinking a cup of coffee, when one of the high school kids lipped off about how tough it must be on us older folks to have to work so hard for more than 30 minutes at a time.

Well now, me being the type that never mouths off, I had to break my record and mention something to protect us older people's image.

"It just so happens that if it wasn't for us older people taking a break every now and then, you kiddies would go to missing your naps so much you would get cranky and your dear old mothers would have to come take you home because their tiny babies was being abused."

Well, this got a pretty good laugh from the older ones in the scale house, but it started a discussion that ranged from "old", to being "old and fat", and then to "old, fat, and completely out of shape". Those kids had gone too far.

Now, Jackie (the cowboss) got in on the argument. "There isn't one of you kids could keep up with any of us on your best day. Fact is, the only thing 18 years has done for you is to let you think you know what you're doing. You can't buck more than five bales of hay at any given time and I know for a fact that you can't flank a calf that's more than four hours old. So any time you want to try Bob and Curt and me out, you just let us know."

I thought he was doing pretty good until that part about "you just let us know". And when I heard 'im say that, I got to thinking maybe he was spending too much time alone with his horse.

I mean, you kinda need to show a little sense when you challenge somebody.    And these somebodies he had just challenged, with the exception of two, were high school basketball and track stars. And to be honest about it, I thought every one of 'em was sure-nuff good hands.

Anywho, one of the newer hands got to kidding me about being fat and being so slow they had to plant a post next to me to see if I was moving or not. He was kinda the ring leader for the Captain Crunch Gang, and they was sure liking the way he was putting me down.

But I won that round...by just making a simple statement. "At least I ain't so fat I can't hire out as a cowboy. Shoot, you're so fat you had to hire out to the branding crew, simply because nobody has ever figured out a way to keep a solidified hunk of water in a saddle."

Corporal Crunch got excited. "Ok, that does it. You think you're so slim and trim, you want to run a foot race? Or has all that talking made you tired?"

Jackie answered his challenge for me. "You bet he does! Just name the time and place and he'll show you what running is all about."

At this point, I forgot about Jackie spending too much time with his horse, and I started to figure a way to shut 'im up. But it was too late, the challenge had been made and accepted.

The little fat Yankee said, "Right now and right

here. We'll run fifty yards up that feed alley. I don't want to run any farther because we may have to carry the poor old fat thing back."

Well, we went to that feed alley and prepared for the race.

Steve went to his pickup and brought out a pair of light weight non-skids. When he got to the starting line, he had on his low runners and had his pant legs rolled up. I could tell I was in trouble.

I mentioned that if I had to run in boots he should have to also. I also mentioned that win, lose, or draw, I would always think he was too fat to cowboy. I figured if I could make 'im mad enough, he might forget to run properly and there might be a slight chance that he would fall at the starting line and break his neck.

Until now, Bob had kept pretty quiet and just watched the verbal war grow out of control. But just seconds before the race, he came up to me and said, "Let 'im lead you for the first 20 yards, then blow his doors off." At that, he turned and as he was walking off, he pert' near fell. I couldn't tell for sure whether he was laughing or crying.

Jackie was having a major discussion with the other kids about the use of semi-pro equipment, when I cut in. "Let's get this over with. And if I live through this, I'll get you, Jackie."

Bob and Dougie stepped off what they figured would be 50 yards and sat down on the feed bunk. They would be the official finish line, Mike would be the official starter, and Jackie would be the official judge. We had so many officials, I didn't think we would have anyone to run the race.

The race started.

That little fat Yankee could run better than I figured he could. But the fact that I was keeping up with 'im blew his mind. Out of that whole mess of people there was

18

only two hollering for me. And of course I used that as part of my excuse for losing the race. He only beat me by 10 yards. And I figured I did pretty good since I hadn't run farther than the length of a catch rope in over 15 years.

G.L. Holmes

Not to mention I had zilch for moral support.

The little fat Yankee said, "You did pretty good, and if you would 'ave had on some tennis shoes like me, I probably wouldn't have beat you so bad."

My legs hurt...

For the next few days, I was the subject of some terrible jokes concerning slow fat cowboys, and what was so bad about it was Jackie started most of them.

I put my little brain in gear and started figuring on a way to get revenge. It only took me about two days to get everything worked out, and I had developed a plan to get this race nonsense stopped.

A few days after the race, we were all gathered up in the scale house taking a coffee break, and I was taking all kinds of verbal abuse, when I mentioned that a 50 yard race wasn't really a true test of anyone's speed or endurance.

And I thought we ought to choose up sides and run a relay race.

Since there were nine of us working there, we could have two 4-man teams. Each man would run a quarter of a mile and the losing team would buy cokes for the winners. It would be a fair test of who was in the best shape, and everyone could still be friends.

I wasn't worried about the ninth man, because Bob was over 50 and he had more sense than the rest of us. He volunteered to be the official starter and ambulance driver.

The Captain Crunch Gang went for it.

I also stated that to make it fair for both teams, Jackie should be on one and I should be on the other. I figured that would only be right for each team to have an elderly fat person as its handicap.

Jackie just sat in the corner and glared at me.

The teams were selected. Jackie picked Dougie, his son, the little fat Yankee, Steve, and Mike.

I got Kip (track star), Kinny (same as Mike, cow-boy), and Alturo. Now, rumor had it that Alturo was a wetback, but since it was against the law to work illegal personnel, I really have my doubts that he was a wetback.

The race was set for the next day.

The next afternoon I had my tennis shoes ready and was all set to run for the cokes. Since the little fat Yankee and me had a grudge, we would start the race. Kip would run against Dougie and Kinny would run against Mike. We figured to let Alturo run last and that put him running against Jackie.

Jackie figured to run last because by the time it came his turn to run, they would be so far ahead that all he would have to do would be to walk to the finish line.

I thought that was kinda stupid thinking.

**The race was on!!!!**

The little fat Yankee out-ran me by about 20 feet, but Kip made up for it by just barely out-running Dougie. Kinny got out-run by Mike just enough to give Jackie a pretty good lead. And from there things just run plumb out of proportion.

Alturo let Jackie have 40 yards on 'im and then made his move. Alturo was running in cowboy boots that were about two sizes too big and they were run down at the heels. So in order to make up for this disadvantage, he not only caught Jackie, but when he passed 'im, he turned around and started running backwards.

To add insult to injury, Alturo lit a cigarette and motioned for Jackie to come on. (This move did not set well with our worthy opponents.)

While Jackie and Alturo were having their match, Dougie was having a fit, a screaming fit. He was a little upset because his dear old dad had a 40 yard lead and then lost it.

After the race was over, Jackie (between long breathless periods) tried to explain what happened. And that he was just tickled pink to have made it to the finish line. Not to mention just to be alive.

The rest of us rode in the ambulance to the finish line and Bob commented that he had never seen anything so pitiful in his life.

When I asked 'im what was so pitiful, he looked at me and grinned and said, "You trying to light a cigarette, and Jackie just trying to stand up."

After everyone finally got their air back, Dougie and Steve went to town and got some cokes. And as we were drinking our prizes, you would never have guessed that anyone had ever mentioned fat or out of shape.

It was agreed on by everyone that the next person to mention a race would have to clean out the dipping vat with a coffee can and a toothbrush.

## Chapter Four
# Custom Cat Castrators: A Non-Profitable Organization

One spring day, as Terry, Larry and I, three school kids, were hanging around the pool hall on our lunch hour, we were discussing our financial crisis.

We had just spent our allowance for the next two hundred years replacing an outhouse that had disintegrated due to careless handling of four stolen sticks of dynamite, three blasting caps, one can of black powder, and five gallons of kerosene. We didn't blow it up on purpose, but no one seemed to believe us.

After we got beat pert' near to death, we had to make arrangements to pay for it. It didn't matter that it hadn't been used in fifteen years. It had to be replaced.

It wasn't our fault that lightning hit our storehouse. And we never did figure out how they knew it was us three that had got the explosives.

But the situation was, we were dead broke and everyone in town was watching us like we had the plague.

We had decided there was no way to get ahead money-wise, so we planned to learn how to play 42 for fun and profit. We were watching ever so close when Elmo Carstead casually mentioned there were just too many cats around the store, the garage and pool hall. He also stated that if he killed 'em off, the mice and rats would soon take over. So there he was, he just didn't know what he was gonna do.

Buel Addleman came up with the perfect solution.

"Elmo, that ain't no problem, all you got to do is castrate the toms, and that way you don't lose any cats, but you don't gain any cats either." Buel never missed a play.

Elmo came back by stating that he didn't have time to catch and castrate those toms, 'cause when he wasn't waiting for an important phone call, he had to be at the pool hall defending his championship. But he admitted that the idea was worth thinking on.

Buel bid 84 and mentioned that since everyone at the pool hall would benefit from such good animal control, they could all chip in some money and pay, oh, fifty cents per tom. That is, if the job was **done right**, you know, no excessive bleeding and things like that.

Well, Terry and I had done started figuring. We figured there must be sixty or sixty-five toms out of that whole town full of cats.

Larry, being the only one showing any sense, started slipping towards the door.

Terry got 'im stopped and started convincing 'im about how easy it would be. After all, we had helped castrate calves, colts, pigs, and sheep. And besides, how else could three fifth grade kids get rich quicker?

Terry was busy with Larry while I was busy trying to get us hired on as custom cat cutters. It took quite a bit of talking. Buel wasn't real sure we had the experience to handle a job as important as this, and Elmo just wanted it done right.

After some pretty hard talking on my part, Elmo and Buel finally gave in, and we sealed the deal.

Elmo said he would put out some scraps in the old cement silo of his. Since it only had one door, he figured he could trap maybe thirty-five or forty cats, and the next day we could skip lunch and come right on over and make ten to fifteen bucks right quick.

He winked at Buel and the deal was set.

We went on back to school and never said a word about our new money making business. That night we all got our pocket knives sharpened to perfection. We know that the sharper the knife, the quicker the cut, and the quicker the cut, the more money we could make.

The next morning at recess we got together and decided that a business of this importance deserved our full-time attention. So we skipped out and headed for the pool hall.

We found Elmo and Buel hard at work, keeping their championship, and convinced them that we wouldn't get into any trouble for skipping classes. After all, school was for kids too dumb to make any money, and besides, we already had our own business. And we had decided that after we cut all the local cats, we just might go from town to town, as professionals.

Well, we followed Elmo and Buel out to that old silo, and when they opened that door, I swear I'd never seen so many cats in my life. It looked like there were a hundred in that little room, and we figured that at least half of 'em were toms.

Elmo and Buel were grinning.

We figured they were just happy to have found someone to do the job. Boy, if we'd only known why they were so happy!

Elmo said that part of the silo was gone, and when they shut us in there, there would be plenty of light to see by.

And when we got done with all the cat cuttin', just holler and they would come let us out. (BULL)

When we stepped into that silo and they closed the door, it dawned on all three of us that we didn't know beans about cuttin' cats.

Now, these cats were a long ways from being gentle housecats, and there probably weren't two in the whole place that had ever been touched by a human. But we didn't think about that, 'cause we were too busy listening to all that hissing and growling. You'll never know what stark cold fear is until you are locked in a silo with a bunch of cats that are as scared as you are.

We seriously discussed going back to school, but we changed our minds on that, because if we went back failures, we were sure to get into trouble. So we decided to just go ahead and get started.

Since I generally had the sharpest knife, it was decided that Terry and Larry would do the flanking. We got started with Terry grabbing a big yeller tom, and from that moment on things just kinda went down hill.

We figured that holding cats was probably like holding calves, once you get a-holt on one, you just don't turn 'im loose. But we also discovered that turning a mad, scared cat loose, wasn't all that easy.

I didn't realize a cat could wreck so much stuff with two stout kids holding him.

Well, they got 'im stretched out, and I cut 'im.

Did you know that when you cut a scared cat, it changes his voice immediately and at the same time his kidneys kinda go crazy? Now, the sound that old cat made, kinda made our hair stand on end, but all that water flying around kinda made it all lay back down again.

Well, I announced that I was through with the surgery, and they could turn 'im loose. I'll guarantee you one thing, folks, turning that cat loose took a way yonder longer than it did to catch 'im.

Seemed like he was holding a grudge.

Did you know a fresh-cut cat can scratch three kids (each one trying to escape) ninety-six times apiece while screaming, and never draw a breath?

26

G.L. Holmes

Now, three kids tryin' to get away from a cat in a silo is a pretty fair wreck, but trying to run from one cat and stay away from ninety-nine more (which by now had gone as crazy as the one just cut) is plumb dangerous.

I don't know if it was Terry or Larry that ran through the door, but I'll love who ever did it forever.

Relief comes in strange forms.

When it was all said and done, we gathered ourselves up and took stock. There wasn't a place on any of us that didn't have a cat track of some kind on it. None of us had a shirt left, they were just threads hanging around our necks and off our shoulders. When we finally calmed down a little, we looked back at that silo and there were cats still coming out of it.

We decided to call our folks instead of going back to school, mainly 'cause the way we were hurting from those cat tracks, it wasn't gonna make any difference who whipped us. There was no way we were gonna hurt any more than we already did.

We had to do a ton of explaining to our folks about the scratches and why we didn't have any shirts left and why we skipped school. Elmo and Buel not only had to explain to three mad moms; they had to give up their chairs in the pool hall for a while.

Seems as though a couple of mothers threatened to kill 'em if they were to be seen around town for a while.

Terry, Larry and I didn't get a whipping, our dads figured the cat tracks would be punishment enough.

But they did offer to beat us to death if we ever skipped school again.

The next time Larry and Terry and I got together, we decided that we would store our next batch of explosives behind the pool hall and hope for another electrical storm.

Come to think of it, we never got our 50 cents for cuttin' that cat.

## Chapter Five
# Bull Cuttin' at the Half-High Pens

Very few people have ever taken the time to stop and appreciate the fact that cowboys go through a lot just so's they can have decent beef to eat. You know the type of beef I'm talking about: the sure-nuff good, not too fat, just right marbling, the full-flavored type.

Now, I was told when I was just a button that the reason the ranchers cut all their bull calves was because as the steer got older, he devoted all the use of his groceries to developing meat, not some kind of body building course to impress the ladies.

And you gotta admit, it makes sense. Without all that extra weight hangin' around distracting him from his official duties of eating, a steer just does a little better.

I've eaten bull beef a time or two, and I could sure tell the difference. Seemed like it had a lot more grease and had a little ranker taste, not the lite kinda taste that steer beef had.

Now, in my short lifetime, I have had the job of using the knife on several occasions. And even though I wasn't all that crazy about the job at times, I could see the advantage.

The advantage being, if I was doing the cutting, I generally got to keep most of the objects that I was cutting out. And of course this meant there would be some pretty good eating, either that evening or in a few days after I had managed to store up a fairly good sized batch of the highly treasured Mountain Oysters.

Working in a feed yard on a processing crew was about the only place the above mentioned job situation would work, mainly because on most of the ranches I've been on, everything was generally saved so that everyone on the crew could have a shot at 'em when suppertime came.

This held true on most cow and calf operations, but when the rancher ran imported cattle, such as Louisiana Selects or Florida Beefmakers, there were generally enough calf fries to go around. Or it was generally agreed upon that everything should be saved until all the cow work was over and there would be one big calf fry and bean eating.

Well, I had hired out to this rancher up in Northeastern New Mexico for the summer, just to straighten out some of those high-dollar Louisiana Selects. The agreement was that these steers would come to me processed and all I had to do was to straighten them out and take care of the poor old things.

That wasn't too bad of an arrangement, considering the fact that I would be getting to rope quite a bit, and I did have a couple of young horses that I wanted to get going.

Well, everything went along pretty good for about three weeks, then one afternoon as I was getting back to camp, I saw my fearless leader's pickup and gooseneck trailer coming down the road.

It was Martín Ochoa, the general fixit man on the ranch, and he was bringing me some more steers.

When I finally got to the pens, he had already unloaded 16 head and was getting ready to pull out for another load. I got 'im shut down and asked what the deal was.

He told me the boss had bought 34 head at the Amarillo sale and had everything processed at the sale barn, then sent to the headquarters. Instead of driving them the 17 miles up to my camp, he just had Martín haul 'em up in the gooseneck.

This in itself was a major break in the ranching industry, especially when you consider that the old boy I was working for thought that the use of any motorized equipment on a ranch was the start of a Communist plot to overthrow the Western United States.

I'm not saying the old man was tight, but his neighbors considered him highly conservative.

I told Martín that when he got back with the next load of steers, I would have supper ready and we could visit for a while before he went back to headquarters.

This pleased Martín for two reasons: one, we both were batchin' and didn't have all that much time to waste visiting; and two, the reason he'd left Mexico was that he was the worst cook in the whole country.

So I turned my horse loose and did my chores. Then I started to turn the new arrivals into a small trap that I usually kept my chronic cattle in. I figured I could hold all of 'em in there for the night, then move 'em out to the first pasture the next morning.

As I started to push the new steers through the gate, looking for signs of sickness or cripples, I noticed that the steers weren't steers.

I did a double-take. Out of the 16 head Martín had unloaded, 14 were bulls. This kinda made me mad, because I was by myself most of the time and pretty busy all the time. And I didn't want to take time to cut some bulls that some idiot at the sale barn didn't.

But I put 'em in the trap and went in to start supper and wait for Martín to get back with the rest.

I figured on checking the next bunch, and if there were more bulls, I would just keep 'em all together until I had time to cut 'em. What I didn't notice was that the two steers had been cut long enough for them to be completely healed up.

When Martín got back with the second load of so-called steers, I went out to check 'em and see if the guys at the sale barn had forgotten all of the bulls or just part of 'em.

It seemed as though they had forgotten all of them.

I got a little huffy and mentioned to Martín that the boys at the sale barn had gotten a little careless with their work orders and hadn't cut but two of the bulls.

He said he noticed 'em when the truck driver had unloaded 'em at the headquarters pens, but he had just figured the boss wanted me to cut 'em, since there wasn't but 32. And I had a lot of extra time, since I had gotten most of the first 1700 head straightened out.

I told Martín that since he figured I had so much free time, I would trade jobs with 'im and I could ride around in the pickup all day, checking fence and water holes.

He told me that if he had wanted to get a job riding horses, he would go to a big city like New Jork and work as a policeman. We just laughed about it because neither one of us really had enough daylight time to get all the things done that needed to be done. So we went to the house and ate supper.

While we were cleaning up the dishes, I mentioned that I didn't know when I would get time to cut those stupid bulls, for at least another two weeks, or maybe longer. I had most of the new cattle straightened out, but it was about time for some of them to break again and there was a good possibility that I would be pretty busy for at least another three weeks. But I would get to 'em as quick as I could. So he could tell the old man not to worry, I'd get it done as quick as I could.

Now, I had worked for this old man a couple of different times and after the first season, there might be as much as two months go by that I didn't see him.

He knew how I worked and I knew what he wanted. So there just wasn't all that much need for him to come around. He would bring my mail and groceries to Martín and Martín would bring the supplies to me, along with any change of plans the old man thought I needed to know.

Well, Martín left and it was almost a week and a half before I saw 'im again. Seems like everything had gone just about perfect for both of us and we got finished for the day about 3:00 in the afternoon.

He got to my camp as I was unsaddling my horse and I figured I'd invite 'im to supper and have someone to visit with.

Then I remembered the bulls.

I remembered how much he liked calf fries and I used this to my advantage. When I suggested that he help me cut all those bulls, I baited 'im with the promise of fresh calf fries, beans and cobbler for supper. Well, he took the bait, and I caught one of my colts. We headed for the pens.

He almost backed out when I told 'im how we were gonna do it.

The instructions went like this. "I'll pen 'em in the big pen, then we can cut five or six out and put 'em in that small pen on the west side. Then I'll heel one, drag 'im to ya, you tail 'im over and hold 'im. Then I'll step off my horse, let him work the rope and I'll cut the bull. I won't take anything but both heels, so it won't be hard on you.

Well, I finally got 'im convinced that was the only way to do it, not using that cowboy-killing chute. Besides that, the colt I was riding needed to get some logging practice.

The bull cuttin' commenced.

Everything went pretty smooth, and a lot quicker than I really figured it would, until we got down to the last three.

There was this big black "Bramer-cross" that had started getting a little wild after we cut out the first two bunches, and he had gotten a lot wilder the farther down the line we went.

Now, Martín was sure trying to convince me to put this one in the chute instead of making the dumb black thing any wilder. But I wouldn't have any part of it. I finally got him in the small pen and attacked.

'Course, when I attacked, so did he. When I made a move to rope his heels, he made a move to throw my colt out of the pen.

Most people know that when a cow critter hooks a horse in the flanks, the horse usually puts on a minor show of protest. Well, this colt went about 145 degrees past "minor" and directly into major.

He went to bucking and pert' near run over Martín and throwed me off right in front of the stupid thing that caused the wreck in the first place.

Back then I was a lot younger and I was used to being treated fairly rough. I didn't mind that old bull calf hitting my horse and making 'im buck. And it didn't bother me all that much for that colt to buck me off. But that goofy black bull jumping up and down on top of me was starting to make me mad.

Now Martín was doing his best to help. He was screaming his lungs out from the top of the fence, and I might add, he wasn't doing all that much good.

I finally got that goofy bull off of me and caught my
horse up, and then I headed for the black varmit that had
done made me mad.

I roped both heels and jerked 'im down.

Then it seemed like I was another 15 minutes talking Martín down off the fence so's he could hold 'im while
I took great pleasure in the rest of my job.

Martín took great pleasure and pride in the fact
that he was very good at windmilling and taking care of
the general maintenance on this ranch, but to say he was

not dedicated to the neutering of the elusive bovine beast in its semi-natural habitat, would be somewhat of an understatement.

I guess you could say he just wasn't all that crazy about sitting on old blackie's shoulder and holding his front leg. I stepped off the colt, when Martín finally got a-holt of the bull, and the proceedings commenced to begin.

After I had removed the protective covering from the objects of my attack, I felt a lot of warm air in my left ear. All motion stopped. I very slowly turned my head to see where the warm air was coming from, and when I saw the source, I started getting really nervous.

It seemed as though the colt really wanted to learn the proper way to castrate bulls. Yep, he had turned around and walked up to my shoulder to see what was going on.

Now, I had my left leg braced against the bull's hind legs, and Martín was sittin on the shoulder, holding the bull's front leg.

Martín had his eyes closed and his teeth gritted, knowing that at any moment that black bull was going to get 'im. (Little did he know.)

I didn't know if I should go ahead and cut the bull or warn my flanking crew, or what. Actually, it didn't take all that long to make a decision.

The bull sensed he was loose and calmly kicked me in the head. When he kicked me, Martín looked around to see what was happening and received a complimentary hind foot to the jaw.

Well, Martín was out cold and I was trying to sneak up on that colt without attracting too much attention from a really upset black almost-steer. When I happened to look around, I noticed the old man was standing outside the pens and he appeared to be just a tad upset.

I figured he might be worried about Martín.

36

**WRONG.**

Seems like he had bought them bulls for a man that produced a few rodeos, and he was gonna pasture them till next spring. Then they would buck 'em out and keep the ones with some promise.

Then he wanted an explanation as to why I was roping them instead of running them through the chute. (I personally thought that was a dumb question.)

After we got Martín woke up, the bull in the chute, and the operation finished, I told the old cuddly thing that all was not lost, because we still had two bulls left.

That didn't help all that much.

What didn't help more than anything was the fact that the two that were left were the two steers that came on the first load.

Martín and I didn't have calf fries for supper that night. Fact is, it was two weeks before we got to enjoy the rangeland delicacies.

But as we discussed all the bruises we acquired and all the screamin' and hollerin' the old man did, we figured it was worth it.

## Chapter Six
# The Not-So Perfect Breakfast

This is the heartwarming tale of how a newly married couple made a decision that would affect the rest of their lives. It wasn't a major decision but it was one that kept her cooking and him a little less mouthy.

It all started out when I took a second job while working at a feed yard in the Texas Panhandle. We were trying to get a house trailer paid off and get a few things extra that weren't really necessary, but while we were thinking of 'em we thought we might as well have 'em.

You know the kinda things: boots, clothes, insurance payments, and an occasional trip to the grocery store.

Now, as I have often said before, the Little Woman is probably the best cook west of the Mississippi. And I say this because I have eaten a lot of food in a lot of different places, not so much fancy food, but general ranch-type groceries. And that's pretty much the type of groceries that the Little Woman cooks. And to go along with the general style of ranch cuisine, she can bake just about any kind of sweets that a man would like to eat.

Due to the fact that the feedlot job wasn't paying enough, I took a second job over at the sale barn of an evening. This job consisted of dipping cattle. And it was supposed to last from 5:00 in the afternoon till midnight. But for about half the time it lasted till one or two in the morning and sometimes till just about time for me to go to work at the feed yard. After about two weeks, I was staying sleepy most of the time. In fact, I was so tired that I couldn't hardly get up of a morning to go to my first job.

So the Little Woman started letting me sleep in until the last minute, simply because I needed every bit of sleep I could get.

Now, you have to understand that at this particular time in my life, I could eat a hindquarter of beef and all the fixin's at a one meal setting. It wasn't greed or gluttony, it's just that it took a lot just to fill me up.

So when it came time for my groceries of a morning, the Little Woman really fixed some groceries.

The breakfast menu was generally pretty simple: 12 eggs, three to six slices of ham or bacon, biscuits, gravy and plenty of coffee. Not to mention some syrup and butter to help satisfy my sweet tooth.

After a couple of weeks, I was getting to the point of rum-dum, and to say I was a little tough to get out of bed of a morning would be an understatement. But the Little Woman stayed tough and we managed for me to hold both jobs.

Then one morning it all caught up with me. The Little Woman had a little trouble getting me up and ready for work.

Now, I'm gonna tell you this much, when I say I will be there, I'll be there. In my whole life I'll bet there haven't been half a dozen times that I haven't shown up when or where I was supposed to. And it was starting to look like this particular day was going to be one of those times. But the Little Woman had made up her mind I was going to get up and after cooking a good breakfast, she finally got me out of bed and got me dressed.

It was a 15 minute drive to the feed yard, and if I really hurried, I had just enough time to wolf down my breakfast and get to work on time. And that's when I kinda made a mistake.

As I stumbled into the kitchen, I noticed that I was in a really bad mood. And I will argue even to this day that what I said wasn't intended to sound near as sarcastic as the Little Woman thought it did.

You need to remember that I wasn't really in my right mind, and she shouldn't have taken it to heart, but she did. And I regretted it as soon as she threw my breakfast out to the dogs.

When I sat down at the table, I made one little comment, just one. That little comment not only cost me breakfast that morning, but it was three years, eight months and twenty-nine days before I had another breakfast.

Now I'll agree I should have taken into consideration that she had been up for a couple of hours, cooking and getting things ready for me just so's I could sleep late and not have to worry about doing the chores. But by gosh, I was pretty tired and still just about asleep, and she should have considered that.

All I said was, "Man, if there's anything I can't stand, it's cold eggs."

It was quite a while before she cooked another breakfast, and when she served it, as far as I was concerned, it could have been ice cubes on toast and I sure wouldn't have said anything about it being cold, or even cool.

## Chapter Seven
# Sewer Problems Can Save Your Marriage

There are quite a few people who honestly believe that marriage is the only thing that has made most men what they are today.

It doesn't make any difference if the old boy is sorry or near-perfect. If it wasn't for his wife, he would be worse off than ever.

Now, there isn't a doubt in my mind that getting married makes an old kid want to settle down and do better. But — when he gets put under pressure, he has a tendency to balk. When I say balk, I mean **balk**.

When the Little Woman and I first got married, it only took me a couple of minutes to realize that marriage wasn't all it's cracked up to be. I learned this as my new wife and I were walking out of the church and heading for my pickup. I'm not sure which old bat said it, but it went something like this:

"I'm so glad he finally got married! Now maybe he'll settle down and sell all those horses and get this silly cowboying out of his head. She will certainly help change him, and the wonderful thing about it is, it can only be for the better. But we'll be able to stop by from time to time and give her a few pointers. I just hope this marriage thing doesn't go in reverse and he brings her down to the same standard that he thinks is so great."

Well, we got off to a fine start. No time for a honeymoon, too many cattle to look after. We had been married for almost 36 hours when we had our first minor discussion.

Actually, I knew it was coming. From the way things had gone that day, it was inevitable. I had been bucked off twice, run over by a steer that was too weak to walk 40 feet to water, and then on the way to the house, I had two flats on the stock trailer.

And to add to the finish, when I got to the house, we had company.

Yep, it was a perfect reception. Two of the Little Woman's aunts and my mother. The air was thick. I wasn't good enough for their niece, and she **might** be good enough for her son. A really comfortable situation.

Of course, my state of mind put the icing on the cake.

By the time I got the horses turned loose and everything fed, I was ready to eat. When I walked in, I noticed there wasn't anything ready to eat. And I casually asked why.

The Little Woman was a little edgy, to say the least. She knew there was no love lost between her aunts and my mother, and all she was trying to do was get along with everyone. Myself, I couldn't have cared less. I was hungry, and I mentioned it.

My mother said if I would get home at a decent hour, I might have a meal ready, and of course the aunts sided with her. The Little Woman just stepped back out of the way.

I told them if the Little Woman hadn't had company all day, she could have had supper on the table. And if they wanted to, they could all come back after I had eaten and gone to bed.

Well, that took care of the company, but there was still a problem concerning my evening groceries. But for the next few minutes I didn't think about it all that much.

The Little Woman didn't really blow up, she just kinda smoked and hissed. She mentioned that I didn't have to be so ill-mannered to company, especially my mother, and she thought I owed them an apology.

I told her that since it was my house, I didn't feel I owed them anything, in fact they owed me. After all, it was my supper they had messed up and I didn't want to hear any more about it. Then I asked her if it was gonna take her all night to fix my supper. Talk about bad timing.

She told me that since it was MY house and MY supper, I could fix it MYself. At that, she pulled a one-woman stampede and went to the back of the trailer house.

I had been warned about trying times such as these, and I had been properly schooled on how to handle the situation. I never gave it much thought, but the ones passing out all the free information were divorced or single.

I squalled, "I'll fix my supper, woman, I'll fix it down at the cafe!"

About the time I got the pickup started, she opened the door on the other side and got in. She said that since I was going to fix my supper down at the cafe, I could fix hers too. We both got gentle and decided that fighting over something like kinfolks just wasn't worth it. And it wasn't, but for the next several months, we had plenty of chances.

Finally we couldn't stand it any longer, we had to get away from kinfolks. So I hired out to a man who had just bought a ranch over close to the Texas border. It was only a 150 mile move, but we figured the distance would at least slow 'em down a little.

44

We sold our house trailer, bought some furniture, and proceeded to move away from the family.

Now, this move was the first for us, and in 19 years of marriage, this one move set a pattern that has yet to be broken. We have changed locations five times in 19 years and have followed the same rules each time. We know it's gonna happen, there isn't any way to avoid it, so we just accept it and wait for it to happen.

We have a fight. Not just a minor disagreement, but a shor-'nuff down and out discussion.

We loaded up my horses and all my horse gear and took everything to the ranch. What we saw when we got there wasn't quite what the man had said it would be.

He said it had a two-bedroom house. It did, if you wanted to put an extra bed in the kitchen.

He said the house had a big kitchen. It did, if you didn't put a couch and chair in the living room.

He said it had all new plumbing. It did, after I spent three days cutting and threading pipe.

He said it had electricity. He lied.

The Little Woman got a little upset.

I tried to explain it wouldn't be so bad after we got settled in, but she wasn't going for it. I finally convinced her things would be alright, when I mentioned that with a small place like that, even if the kinfolks came to visit, they wouldn't stay long.

The only nice part of the deal was there was a big bath tub and shower. Whoever added the bathroom on to this overrated lean-to had done a good job.

After about two weeks of fixing and replacing, we were finally moved in and ready to receive cattle. 'Course, when you're ready to receive cattle, you're ready to receive kinfolks.

The kinfolks got there a couple of days before the cattle did, a whole car load of 'em.

Since they didn't come to see me, I tried to stay busy down at the horse pens, but that didn't work.

It seems that all those visitors kinda over-taxed our bathroom drain system, mainly from the toilet section. It hadn't drained right since we had been there, and all the extra use was just too much for it.

It kinda stopped up, backed up, and just plain quit working.

The Little Woman came down to the pens and explained the situation to me. Even though our guests weren't going to spend the night, they would probably wait till late to leave, and since it was still pretty early in the day, we had just as well try and get it fixed.

I mumbled something about acres of mesquite brush and milk weed leaves, but when I noticed the look in her eye, I backed off.

One thing I had learned in the 11 months of blissful marriage was when to be boss and when to be straw-boss. And this was definitely one of the straw-boss times.

I went to the house with the Little Woman in hopes of solving the drain problem. FAT CHANCE!

Things were looking pretty bleak for me. I couldn't make anything work like it should, and the lye was just setting there bubbling. I was getting mad and desperate. Then I had what had to be the greatest idea I have ever come up with.

A few days before, when I was trying to find where the sewer line ran to, I found a half inch nipple with a cap on it, welded to the sewer line. The sewer line being a three inch galvanized pipe, meant it could stand a little pressure. The butane tank was only a few feet away from the sewer line and I had enough hose to reach the nipple with the cap on it.

I shut off the butane, rigged a hose to the nipple, then went inside and told everybody not to smoke or light any kind of fire. Then I told one of the aunts to grab a plunger and work on the toilet while the Little Woman worked on the bathtub drain.

I headed for the butane tank. I figured if I hooked the line from the nipple direct to the tank and by-passed the regulator, we could get enough pressure to blow everything out of the sewer line.

Boy, was I ever right!

When I hollered was everybody ready, and they hollered back that they were, I opened the valve on the butane tank as fast as I could. Nothing happened for a couple of seconds, but when it did happen, it happened all at once.

The line blew clear. 'Course it blew clear *towards the house* a couple of seconds before it blew the lid plumb off the septic tank. About the time the lid hit the trunk of our guest's car, I heard some of the wildest screamin' and cussin' I have ever heard in my life, especially from women.

When I got the butane shut off, I ran to the house. What I saw was not a pretty sight: two of the nastiest looking women I had ever seen. What I heard was some of the nastiest names I had ever heard any living thing being called.

Have you ever tried to escape two man-hating women while crawling on the floor, trying to get your breath and stop laughing all at the same time?

Yep, it was a terrifying experience. There were babies crying, women screaming, and dogs barking on the porch, and one thoroughly messed up bathroom.

When I finally slowed down on the laughing, I talked the Little Woman and her nasty aunt into going to the storage tank and using the drain valve to wash off. I got her two cousins to take some towels and extra clothes down to 'em, and then I went to check on the bathroom.

It wasn't all that bad, other than the walls and ceiling being a little different color and the toilet setting in the bathtub. And the smell was slightly awful. Butane and old sewer contents just don't mix all that well.

The unwanted aunt gathered up her brood as soon as she had wallered into one of the Little Woman's dresses and left. I guess she was a little upset. She didn't even mention the dent the septic tank lid made when it hit the trunk of her car.

It took some talking, but after we got the bathroom cleaned up and the toilet bolted back in place, the Little Woman finally saw the funny side of it. Not the **big** funny side, the little funny side, and things got back to pert' near normal.

We managed to keep people away just by mentioning we were having trouble with the sewer line. Believe it or not, it even worked at the next couple of places we lived. And as long as we weren't moving or entertaining kinfolks, we got along just fine.

Chapter Eight
# Range Country Remedies:

When I decided to become a cowboy, I wasn't aware of some of the drawbacks that came with the occupation.

Oh, I knew about long hours, the sometimes miserable working conditions, and the fact that you could make more money selling pop bottles, but, I had been raised to accept things not going just the way they should. So I wasn't disappointed about the usual job hazards.

What really did bother me was that 'most everyone in the cow business figured they were some kind of general practical doctor. After my first experience with sickness at a cow camp, I promised myself that should I ever get sick, I would not tell anyone but the first doctor I could get to. And if you want to know a little secret, every time I've broken that promise, I've regretted it.

### Jalapeño Cough Syrup

I was just out of high school and had hired out to a ranch up in the Torrington, Wyoming, country.

When I arrived, there was quite a bit of snow on the ground and a bunch more falling. I had left New Mexico because we'd had a pretty bad winter, and I didn't have enough sense to realize that the farther north you went, the worse the weather got. But I had hired out and I figured I would stay awhile. It was the most cold and snow I had ever seen.

The ranch had two camps for married men and a big bunk house at the headquarters for the single men. I liked everybody in the bunk house but it seemed the help just kept changing. Most of the work involved feeding, and not much cowboying. And with all that snow on the ground, feeding was not a fun job.

After I had been there for about two weeks, the foreman hired an old boy from Florida. He was a drifter and you could tell he hadn't ever done any hard work. But we needed some help on the feed wagons and help was getting hard to find.

He was fat, lazy and he smelled like a wet coyote. All he could do was gripe about the weather and the equipment. The only thing he liked was the food.

Well, after about two weeks of working in the snow and getting a little wet, he caught a cold, and the poor old fat thing really got to complaining.

Now, I had been around some sick people a time or two, but I had never seen anyone who coughed as much as he did, or anyone as helpless. He would just lay around and cough and complain. He coughed so much at night, we couldn't get any sleep.

The foreman offered to take 'im to the doctor, but the old fat thing was afraid the doctor might cure 'im and he would have to go back to work. All of us were wishing he would either get well or die.

During the worst part of the sick man's spell, I managed to get a day off and go to town. Among some of my purchases, I got a couple of cans of jalapeños. I had a craving for some spicy food. And I fully intended to flavor

50

up breakfast the next morning.

When I got back to the ranch that evening, old Bob had had about all of the coughing he could stand. Fact is, he was just about ready to put the old chronic out of his misery. And I believe the other hands would have sworn to the fact that the old lazy thing had just committed suicide.

As I was putting up my new shirt and Levi's, Bob noticed my canned peppers. He came over and offered me two dollars for one can. I may be a little goofy every now and then, but when I see a chance for a profit, I take it. He paid me, took the peppers, and went to his little room at the end of the bunk house.

After a while, he came out and visited with a couple of the other hands kinda quiet-like. I noticed every now and then one would sneak a peek at the cougher and nod his head. Well, after a five-minute summit meeting, old Bob walked over to the stricken man, holding a medicine bottle with some terrible looking green stuff in it.

He told the cougher he had just found some cough syrup he had forgotten he had. And he thought it would do some good if he took some right away.

The cougher assured Bob that he didn't really need any medicine because he felt like the cold was just about over. Bob and the other hands assured the cougher if he didn't take at least two spoons of the syrup on his own, they would give him the whole bottle with a drench gun. He had his choice, but any way it went, we figured on getting some sleep.

Well, he took the first big spoonful of that weird looking stuff and pert' near had a smothering spell. Before he could get his breath, Bob and another hand had forced the second spoonful down his throat.

I've seen some critters fight their heads before, but never had I seen some of the stuff this old poor thing pulled. I'm telling ya, the man went nuts. He grabbed his throat, fell over backwards, rolled on the floor trying to scream, and headed for the water bucket.

A couple of the hands thought they might have killed 'im, a couple more were hoping they had, and I was holed up at the head of my bunk, hoping he wouldn't try to kill all of us if he lived through whatever had happened to 'im.

When the poor old thing finally got his breath, he wanted to know just what kind of medicine he had been forced to take? And why his throat was burning like a runaway volcano?

Bob told 'im it was just about the best cough syrup money could buy. It contained plenty of jalapeño peppers so as to burn out any infection in his throat and belly, and about 60% mineral oil.

Of course, everyone knew what the mineral oil was for. It was to help the jalapeños slip right on through his system after they had done their job of killing out all those little germs that kept 'im coughing all the time.

Well, the cough syrup went to work almost immediately. Seems that after he found out what was in it, he didn't want to cough. I guess he didn't want to strain any unnecessary muscles during the night.

He didn't sleep much that night, mainly because he spent most of the night in the outhouse, but the rest of us got a pretty good night's sleep, even though every now and then someone would wake up laughing.

### A Miracle Cure for Cowboy Diaper Rash

One time I traded for a saddle with a padded seat. I had ridden this saddle a time or two at a couple of ropings and I just had to have it. I liked it and started using it just about all the time, instead of just for roping.

That was my first mistake. The second mistake was not giving that padded seat time to dry out after it had been rained on for about three weeks early one fall.

Now some of you may have guessed the type of ailment that I developed, but for those of you that have never been in a situation like that, I'll explain. I kinda got a little galled, all the way around from one knee to the other. And it didn't make any difference what I tried, I couldn't clear it up. I had been married about a year and the Little Woman couldn't figure out how to help me out. Of course, I didn't just tell everybody about my tender situation. About the time my little rash started clearing up, it would come another rain and I would start all over again. Some people think they get grouchy when they try to quit smoking. Bull. They ain't seen grouchy.

Well, the Little Woman and I had been invited to a party that was to have plenty of food, drink, and dancing. We both liked to dance and we had figured on going. But the day of the party, things got worse, I mean **big time** worse. I had spent all day sorting steers and getting things straightened out in a couple of pastures that had gotten mixed. It had been hot and muggy all day and me riding a damp saddle and sweating like crazy, my lower area was on fire.

It was hurting so bad I would have cried if I had thought it would help. When I finally got to the house that evening, I was not only hurting, I wasn't in any mood to go dancing. I could hardly walk, much less dance.

Well, I finally got the Little Woman calmed down and told her if she could find something to ease the pain, we would go out.

I will never ever make such a deal again, not even with the Pope. She wanted to go to that dance pretty bad, so bad she caused me to pull a one-man stampede and pert' near drown myself, trying to undo what she had just had me do to myself.

She went through the medicine cabinet, looking for anything that might come close to easing my pain. She found some kind of lotion that had Cali-something in it, and when she read the directions, it said to apply liberally to affected area.

This bottle of lotion was showing signs of being very old and we had no idea where or when we got it, not to mention why. She said it was good for insect bites and stings. Then there was a faded place, and the word "rash".

I told her I would try it.

I went to the bathroom, took off my clothes, and applied liberally to the affected area. I guess I made a lot more noise than I normally do when I take a shower, 'cause when the Little Woman finally got the door open and came inside to see why I was cussin', the unfeeling old bat fell down on the floor laughing.

I guess I did look a little ridiculous, mainly because the affected area was on fire. I couldn't figure out why it wasn't smoking, it was so hot. And I'll tell you something else. It's tough to try and chew somebody out when you're standing on your head in a shower, with cold water running down your chest and into your face. I know 'cause I tried it.

After the fire got down to a slow smolder, I got up the nerve to get dressed, and by the time we got to the party, the Little Woman had just about quit laughing and the affected area was numb.

We never did figure out what that lotion was for, and we haven't seen it in any stores. But I got rid of that bottle and any time I get to feeling poorly or get hurt, I make sure I'm the only one that knows about it.

54

Chapter Nine
# Do-Gooders Don't Always Do That Much Good

Just the other day I was confronted by two ladies from a cat club. At first, I figured they were a couple of lost people, 'cause no one else ever pulls up to our place except bill collectors or some idiot insurance salesman. Since I can spot a bill collector a quarter-mile away, and they just didn't look like salesmen, I just naturally figured they were lost.

As they stopped in front of the house, I left the horse I had been shoeing and walked over to say hello and see if I could help 'em out. (I should've stayed with the horse.)

The conversation went something like this:

"Yes Ma'am, can I help you?"

"Are you Curt Brummett?"

"Yes Ma'am; How much do I owe you?"

"Well Mr. Brummett, you don't owe us anything, but we believe you owe the animals you have abused and mistreated a great deal more than you could ever repay."

Each word had enough venom dripping off of it to supply all the rattlesnakes in Eastern New Mexico and West Texas for life. I decided right quick I wouldn't invite 'em in for coffee.

I've always been pretty hot-headed and prone to get myself whipped simple because I would blow smooth up and attack when I got mad. But I figured I would get in a lot more trouble from dottin' this old bat in the eye than I would if I just let her rattle on. Besides that, this was my place and I could just tell 'em to leave.

"We are not here in an official capacity; we are just here to get an explanation for the way you seem to like to treat animals, cats in particular, Mr. Brummett." She said this as she unloaded from her car.

It was one of those foreign cars and when she unloaded, the springs gave a sigh of relief as they came back to a semi-normal position. The other old gal started to get out too.

The first lady was about fifty to fifty-five and big. She had the coldest green eyes I had ever seen, and she was wearing Levi jeans and a khaki shirt. She was even wearing combat boots! (Actually they were hiking boots.) Her hair was kind of a blood bay and fixed pretty nice. But she was as big as I am and moved like a tank.

I wasn't scared, though, because I still had my shoeing hammer in my hand. I figured if things got plumb out of hand I could always use it on myself to end all the pain this old gal looked like she could inflict on me.

Her pardner came around the front of the car.

She looked like she could be twenty to thirty-five and stood about five feet-six. She was dressed about the same way as her friend, and her hair was cut short. Now I'm not saying the woman was ugly, but if she had been inclined to a military career, she could have been a three-star general in the Canine Corps.

I gripped the hammer a little tighter.

They introduced themselves and then started demanding explanations.

During all of this I was racking my brain trying to

figure out what they were talking about. I finally got 'em shut down and told 'em to talk one at a time and tell me just what it was I was supposed to have done that was so terrible.

The big one, I'll call her Moose, took a step toward me and pointed her finger.

I raised the hammer a little.

"We heard about your cat castrating. When we came to talk to you about it, we had to ask directions as to how to get here. We stopped at the service station to ask where you lived, and visited with two very nice men. They not only told us how to find your house; they even explained how they have been trying for years to get you to give up your cruel ways. They even donated $5.00 apiece to our organization and told us how good they thought we were for coming out here to try and get you to stop these terrible things."

Mike and H. L. were the first two to come to my mind. I chanced a look over my shoulder and sure 'nuff, there was Mike's pickup settin' on top of the hill. I would've bet everything I owned they were sittin' on the hood, each with a pair of field glasses and probably a cold beer.

Them's two sick people.

I made up my mind that if I lived through this, I would get even.

I explained that I hadn't even touched a cat in twenty years, and that the only cat I ever cut lived to scratch the clothes off of three kids. And as far as being cruel to animals, I would try to show them I wasn't. If they liked, I would show them around my place and let them judge for themselves.

After a quick tour of the horse pens and the chicken house and speaking to each of the eight dogs, they had calmed down considerable. Then it happened.

Three of those pups and one big brown cat made

their appearance, the pups running in hot pursuit of the cat.

Now, this old brown cat had been hanging around my horse pens and hay stacks for about two years. He sure helped keep the mouse problem under control and most of the birds out of the garden. But he always stayed out of sight. In fact, I hadn't even seen 'im or thought of 'im in two or three weeks. But, of course, he had picked today to show up.

I knew what he was gonna do, and those older dogs knew what he was gonna do. The only ones in the dark were the three pups and those two goofy women.

The General screamed, "We've got to help that poor kitty. Those mean dogs will chew her to pieces."

Moose broke into a run to head off the dogs, and the General headed for the poor kitty.

The rest of those dogs figured if those two woman could run the cat, then they might just have a chance to whup that poor kitty once and for all. And all eight dogs joined the chase.

This particular cat was probably the toughest critter in all of Eastern New Mexico, and seven counties in West Texas. He weighed about twenty to twenty-five pounds and had single-handedly whupped every dog that had ever showed up in our little town. His favorite trick was what he was trying to work this morning.

If he happened to get bored, he would stroll around until he got the attention of some new pup or aggravate one of the older ones until he had an all-out chase goin'. He would run these pups all over the place — around the horse pens, the hay stack, and the roping chute, and then he would head for the middle of the arena. When he got to his spot, he would turn and proceed to whup the stuffings out of whatever was chasing 'im.

By the time Moose and the General had got lined

out, the cat had made it to the arena. The only problem was, this time when he turned around, he saw a little different situation. From his reaction, I would say he wasn't really scared, just a little confused. He not only had every dog on the place coming for 'im, but he had a huge person closing in on the dogs and a two-legged pit bull closing in on him.

I know in my own mind he figured he could handle the dogs, but the Moose and the General were just too much to put up with.

He sold out, but just a hair too late.

The General had cut across, and just as the cat turned, the General grabbed 'im.

Yep! It was a terrible sight. And the sounds weren't all that pretty either.

The cat proved what I had thought ever since he had showed up — he didn't like to be handled.

About the time the General picked kitty up, she scared 'im pretty good. The first thing kitty did was to put a lip lock on the General's arm. This in turn caused a scream similar to that of a gut-shot werewolf.

The scream made the dogs think the cat was hurt and could probably be whupped pretty easy, so they attacked. The Moose thought the dogs hurt the cat, and she attacked. The General knew the cat wasn't hurt, and all she wanted was loose.

Seemed from where I stood, the General had had about all the rescue work she wanted.

Now, as most people know, when a cat feels that his life is in danger, he climbs. It's his natural instinct. It doesn't make any difference what it is — he's gonna climb, he's just gotta climb. Well, this cat figured since he was already up off the ground, he might as well stay there. So he dug the old claws in and tried to ride the storm out.

By now, the General had developed an entirely

different attitude concerning where that cat should be. She pulled 'im loose and gave 'im to the Moose.

This evidently pleased the cat because he climbed the Moose's pants leg, went up her back, and settled on her head. And I might add this was no easy accomplishment.

For a large person, the Moose moved pretty good. She was kicking dogs, slappin' at that cat, and using a strange language. By the time that cat reached the top of his new tree, I was about there and was fixin' to start kickin' dogs. Then a strange thing happened.

The General figured she had better help the Moose and waded right into the middle of all those dogs. A brave move! The General slapped that cat so hard, she not only knocked the cat loose from the Moose but she knocked the wig plumb off the Moose's head. All you could see was two old chunks of hair fly out over the dogs and hit the ground.

Everything got quiet for about five seconds. I mean, all motion stopped.

Those dogs couldn't figure where that "other cat" had come from; the cat couldn't figure out what kinda critter had chased it out of its make-shift tree; the General couldn't figure how she knocked the Moose's head off; and the Moose was trying to figure out why the General hit her instead of the dogs.

The cat was the first to move. He hauled freight and headed for the haystack! The dogs couldn't figure why "the other cat" just laid there, so they attacked.

Those two women looked at each other, started crying, and headed for their car. The Moose was a lot spookier than she had been. I don't care how you look at it, a pert' near bald headed woman that size is spooky. As they ran past me, I noticed neither of them was hurt too bad — a couple of scratches and one or two fang marks, but nothing serious.

By the time they had gotten in their car and left, things had calmed down considerable. I looked around, and the cat was sittin' on top of the haystack, trying to figure out why that funny little furry critter wasn't puttin' up much of a fight. Mike and H. L. were rolling around on the ground, and I could hear them laughing from a quarter-mile away.

The dogs had the wig divided equally, and the pups were prancing around with their trophy, each one figuring they had taught that cat a very important lesson.

I figured since everything was pert' near back to normal, I would just go back to shoeing my horse. I had to wait a while.

You can't shoe a horse when you're laughing.

## Chapter Ten
# Hair Curlers Can be Hazardous to Your Health

Contrary to popular belief, springtime in the sand hills isn't all that much fun. Just because things are greening up and the calves are slick, fat and sassy, it doesn't mean that everything else is hunky dory.

Now don't get me wrong, I enjoy seeing everything green up and all the new calves start growing up, but I'm not all that crazy about a few of the other things that all that nice warm weather brings out.

By "other things" I mean scorpions and yellow jackets.

It had been raining and misting for about three days in a row one spring, and the weather was just a touch cooler than normal. I guess all the cool, damp weather had made a few of the wilder critters hunt some form of protection from the elements.

As I was getting ready to leave out one cool damp morning, the Little Woman suggested I take a jacket, preferably the one I had hung up on the floor by the kitchen door.

I commented that should I decide to take a jacket I would take whichever one I wanted. I said this kinda under my breath as I picked up the jacket and started putting it on. I mean, there wasn't any point in stirring the Little Woman up over something as silly as a jacket.

About the time I started buttoning my jacket, I noticed a slight discomfort along my left arm.

It felt kinda like someone was trying to put out about twenty-seven ceegars, all of 'em in the same spot.

By the time I had ripped off the jacket, knocked the coffee pot off the table, and run smooth over the Little Woman, I had things in a bit of a mess.

G.L. Holmes

Jughead (my Pitbull-Queensland Heeler Crossbred Cowdog pup) took it on himself to protect the Little Woman, and took after me.

It's bad enough to try and put out a range fire on your arm, help the Little Woman up, and fight off an overly protective mutt. But when the one you're helping causes the one you're fighting to fight more, it gets plumb out of hand.

I finally let the Little Woman fall back on the floor, grabbed that idiot dog, threw 'im out the back door, and then started checking on my arm.

As I took off what was left of my shirt, the Little Woman picked up what was left of my jacket and shook out three scorpions. They were big enough to be replacements for any one of those horses that pull the refreshment wagon at state fairs and parades. Fact is, I don't see how I managed to pick up that jacket with those three critters inside it.

My arm was hurting and swelling at the same time. Jughead was still standing at the kitchen door, growling like a big dog, and the Little Woman was in the process of killing the last of the stinging horses.

I'm the type of person who's allergic to ant bites, bee stings, and harsh criticism. I had pills for the first two, but I usually have to find an understanding neighbor to help with the last one. But the way my arm was hurting, I figured I could put up with the uncouth comments from the Little Woman concerning the spilt coffee.

As she gave me my pills, she actually showed some concern, even if it wasn't but for three or four seconds. Then she mentioned that I had better go to the doctor and see if I needed any other kind of medicine.

I agreed. Those pills seemed to help, but I was feeling kinda flighty. I went to start the car while the Little Woman was changing out of her coffee-stained clothes. I thought she picked some strange times to look stylish. She came out the door about the time I finally got the car started and pulled up to the front door.

She had brought me another shirt and made me change while the car was warming up. My arm's swelling up and fixin' to bust, and she's worried about my appearance.

The Little Woman decided since we were going to town anyway, we should take Jughead with us and get his rabies shot. So Jughead got in the back seat, and the Little Woman started driving. It's only about thirty miles to town, but with the Little Woman chewing me out about the coffee and knocking her down, it only seemed about eighty.

As the doctor was giving me a shot, I was trying to explain the teeth marks on my hand. But the sight of a needle kinda made me nervous, so I figured I'd just let the Little Woman handle it. She did.

She said, "Oh, he just gets excited over nothing. And when he does, so does my puppy."

Puppy, my foot! That sucker weighed forty pounds and was still growing.

The doctor mentioned we ought to give Jughead a rabies shot, considering what all he had been chewing on in the last couple of days.

The shot I got from the doctor didn't do much for the swelling, but it sure made me feel better. So I suggested that the Little Woman do some grocery shopping while I took the pup to the vet.

After I let the Little Woman out at the local Safeway, it seemed to me that the heater was working a little too well in that old car. I went to turn it off and that's when I got my first clue that things weren't just what they should be. The heater wasn't on. It had been, but it wasn't now.

About two blocks from the grocery store, Jughead

started snapping and growling. Of course the first thing I thought of was RABIES. I turned around to see what the problem was, and got stung right between the eyes by a kamikaze yellow jacket.

I guess that nice warm air and them smooth New Mexico roads had kinda upset the little critters.

For the moment I forgot about driving and started swatting yellow jackets, while tryin' to find the door latch. Yep, there was a whole herd of those stinging critters, and it appeared that all of 'em were upset.

It was about the same time that the car jumped a curb. The damage wasn't all that bad. Somehow I missed the thirty-one cars (each carrying two to four witnesses) and made it through the stoplight. But I got the sign that was advertising three burritos for ninety-nine cents with the purchase of one gallon of Paula Sue's Special Soda Pop. 'Course the sign was posted on the door of Paula Sue's new Lincoln Town Car.

After the police left, the insurance people left, the yellow jackets left, and I got Jughead calmed down, I called a friend to go pick up the Little Woman and bring her to the scene of the wreck.

I had only been stung three or four times, but I sure did hurt. My eyes were almost swelled shut, and I didn't want to take a chance on getting into another car wreck.

By the time Mike and the Little Woman got there, I was sicker than a poisoned pup. And Jughead had a few whelps on his head. This had not been a good day.

Mike took the pup to the vet and said he would meet us at the doctor's office. And we headed to the shot shop.

Two shots and a thirty minute lecture on never slapping at a bee or yellow jacket later, the doctor said I could go home. He also suggested I stay in bed for a day or two, and give the swelling time to go down.

To say I was getting paranoid about things touching me would be an understatement. I pert' near bailed out of the car a half dozen times because I thought something was crawling on me. I was sure 'nuff spooky.

As we went to bed that night, I noticed the Little Woman's head was considerably larger than usual. She had a pickup load of curlers in her hair and had some kind of bed sheet or tarp holding 'em in place.

No big deal. If she wanted to put herself through that kind of torture just to look good, it was okay with me.

Sometime around 2:30 that morning, I noticed a slight stinging sensation around the small of my back.

I pulled a one-man stampede.

Everywhere I went, that critter followed me. I couldn't seem to get rid of the covers and every time I went up, that critter was under me when I came down. I was slapping the bed, hollering about a fourteen-pound scorpion with six of his kinfolks helping 'im.

Of course this upset the Little Woman just a tad. She's not that easy to get along with when she wakes up on her own and this sudden commotion sure wasn't helpin' her disposition any.

With me making all kinda noise, that goofy pup came into the bedroom to get in on the act.

He did very well for just a puppy.

Since it was dark, he just bit anything that was handy. I don't think the Little Woman would have gotten in such a hurry if he hadn't bit her, but something seemed to inspire her to quicker action.

By the time the Little Woman got a light on, the dog locked out in the hall, and me off the top of the dresser, she had pulled the covers off the bed.

And right there in the middle of that bed, lying in wait for their next victim, were two of the most vicious looking hair curlers I had ever seen.

I blew smooth up.

Very few times have I ever laid the law down, but that night about nine years ago I laid a law down that hasn't been broken yet. And I made it pretty clear.

Should the need arise for the Little Woman to sleep with them spiny little things in her hair, she could do so in the pickup, the barn, or out in the pasture. And when she did, she could take that goofy pup with her.

For pert' near nine years now, when I go to bed each night, I reach over and pat the Little Woman on the head. That's just to make sure that if I roll over on something that stings, I have a good reason to pull a one-man stampede.

## Chapter Eleven
# Female Help, A Universal Problem

The other day, Jim, H.L. and me were sitting around the scale house, drinking coffee and discussing the mainest reasons for all the world problems. And you can believe it or not we were in total agreement on the basic cause of all the really big malfunctions that were causing so much trouble.

Yep, it was a unanimous decision.

The trouble with our little world was women. It seems we all had the same problem concerning women. And that problem was, the silly old things just wouldn't listen. It didn't make any difference what you tried to tell 'em, they just didn't pay any attention. And when it was all said and done, they just went ahead and did what they wanted to any way.

Jim commented on the fact that his wife was a pretty good hand ahorseback, but it took 'im pert' near 15 of their 20 years of blissful marriage to get her trained to the point of doing things right. And he did finally get her far enough along that she could go and neighbor without being an embarrassment to 'im.

Well, H.L. and me could sure understand where he was coming from, because both of us had had our share of wife-training troubles. And old H.L. told 'im he just about had things figured out about teaching women anything. He says if you wanted 'em to learn anything at all, just tell 'em to leave it alone.

H.L. admitted that he hadn't been able to teach his wife anything. And after 15 years of marriage, he just decided to give up and let the poor old cuddly thing just stumble through life the best she could. Then he went into great detail on what made 'im decide to just give up. Here's his story.

### H.L.'s Version

We had taken the car into town to get some scour boluses for some baby calves.

We got back to the pens just as most of the cows were going back to pasture, but there were three pair that I was wanting to look at still at the water trough. So I closed the gate and walked in to check on the calves.

I didn't know what had caused these critters to start scouring so bad but they sure needed some medicine. So I tell Old Cuddles to bring me the pills and that old catch rope I keep in the trunk of the car and I'll just doctor those babies right now while I've got 'em in the pen.

She brought everything, just like I asked her to, and then she told me to cut the calves off in a smaller pen so's the cows wouldn't get excited and I wouldn't have to run the little darlings to death trying to get a rope on 'em. Well the first part of that was okay, 'cause I had figured on doing that anyway, but the second little tidbit concerning my roping was not needed and I didn't appreciate it at all.

I told her not to worry about it, just stay out of the way, and when I got a calf down, to bring me a couple of pills. She throwed that box of pills at me and told me she wasn't getting in the pen with those cows after they had been stirred up, and especially if any or all of them thought one of their calves was in trouble.

I told her if she had any idea as to what she was talking about, it would help, but since she didn't, I would just do it by myself. I then told her that the cows were gentle and there wasn't anything to worry about.

I put the pills in my shirt pocket and roped the first calf. The scours hadn't done anything to weaken the silly thing and it was a little tougher getting him on the ground than I had thought. Of course fighting off his dear old mama took a little time but I finally got two pills down 'im, got the rope off, caught my breath, and headed for the second calf.

By this time, all three cows were getting a little edgy and the calves were acting like their maws. The wife told me to quit being so bull-headed and cut the other two off and doctor 'em separate. I told her that since she wasn't in there helping, to keep quiet and I would do it myself.

The second calf was a little tougher to catch, mainly because all that jabbering the woman had been doing was making 'im nervous, and it took me three loops to catch 'im. He was away yonder more active than the first calf and his mama didn't fight off near as easy. She never actually hit me but she got so close while I was holding her baby down, she stepped on my ankle and soaked my shirt with some really bad smellin' slobbers. When I turned that calf loose, I figured I needed to drink a beer and catch my breath.

As I hobbled over to the fence, I told Jan to get me a beer out of the car, and as I got to the fence, I noticed she hadn't moved. It was about this time I figured out she was a little upset with me. I told her never mind, I'll just doctor that last calf and we'll go on to the house. So I hobbled off across the corral in hot pursuit of the third and final calf.

Now, he was considerable bigger than the first two, and wilder, and he wasted no time in showing a desire to be free. There weren't but about 43 places in that fence that were weaker than the rest, and after about three tries, he found one of 'em. He busted through like there wasn't anything there to begin with, and headed north.

Now, the old gal I had been living with got plumb upset. I told her if she hadn't been hollering so much, that calf wouldn't have got so wild and tore down a fence trying to get away.

I also mentioned that now we had to try and catch 'im, so's we could doctor 'im for the scours and see how bad the cut was on his shoulder.

She wanted to know just how I figured I was gonna do that, since I barely could walk and he seemed to be doing about 30 miles an hour. I told her that if she was half as smart as she thought she was, she would have done figured that out. And then I explained just how simple it really was.

All she had to do was drive the car, I would ride on the hood, and when she got me close enough, I would rope the poor sick critter and that would be that. Well, we started off in hot pursuit.

The calf didn't run all that far before he slowed down and started bawling for mama. That made catching up to 'im pretty easy. I was sitting on the hood and the Little Lady eased up pretty close. The calf suspected something and started off again.

I hollered for Jan to speed up, she did. She gassed the car so much it laid me back on the hood, and just about the time I got set back up and was fixing to throw a loop, she hit the brakes.

I passed that calf on my back and tore up about 200 yards of perfectly good grass. The calf kept right on going.

When she pulled up to me I asked why she had

decided to stop. She said she was afraid she might run over the calf.

Well, the second time around went somewhat smoother. I got the calf caught with the second loop and was in the process of giving it a couple of pills, when all of a sudden it got very dark.

It seems as though during the first chase the calf was calling for mama, and mama was trying to get out to help her baby. During the second chase, somewhere between the first and second loops, Maw got out of the pens and came to the aid of Junior. About the time I got set up and looked around, Maw and Junior were headed off to the draw in the west end of the pasture and Jan was sitting in the car with a silly grin on her face.

After I spit out a dump truck load of dirt and kinda got my breath back, I asked why she didn't warn me about the freight train on legs coming after me. She kept that same silly grin and said she didn't want to holler any more, because it might upset the cows and calves and she sure didn't want to go get 'em any more excited than they already were.

It was right then and there that I made up my mind, that I would never try and do anything like that again. There just ain't no getting any help with a woman around.

I knew just exactly what he was saying. After all, I had tried to teach the Little Woman something about windmills once upon a time.

## Chapter Twelve
# My Dog's a Democrat

Very few people understand why they do some things. I did something a few years back and I figured out why I did it.

I did it for revenge!

I had hired out to this outfit in Eastern New Mexico for the one and only purpose of gathering wild cattle. When I took the job, I had in my possession two real well trained cowdogs and a pup that someone had given me.

When I took the pup, I thought the old boy was really trying to be friendly, but after about three weeks, I realized that there was a possibility that somewhere in a previous life, I must have really made this old boy mad.

The pup he gave me tested my patience. Not just once in a while, but at least 37 times a day, and more if I was trying to teach 'im anything.

He was a good dog, but it was about three years before he could be trusted, and he never did get it through his thick head that I was the boss.

The pup I'm talking about is Jughead. He was my Pitbull-Queensland Heeler Crossbred Cowdog. He was, beyond a doubt, the ugliest, most bull-headed, idiot-styled, most over-fed, under-worked, clabber-mined, self-centered, egotistical, attention-craving dog I have ever owned.

He was also the best.

When things were going like they should, I referred to 'im as Jughead, or Pup. When things were going as they usually did, I referred to 'im in terms that, when put on my typewriter, melted the ribbon.

It was along about the time I received old Jughead, that I was forced to change my political standings.

I had been a registered member of this certain political party ever since I had registered for the first time. I was registered this way simply because my family had always been in it and I didn't see any point in changing.

Very few people realize the kind of political pressure I was under. I guess I was the black sheep of the family, mainly because I thought everything this party did was a complete waste of time, not to mention a waste of the taxpayer's money.

I had old Jughead with me and we were covering some of the sand country in search of some cattle, and we found a two year old bull.

From where we started, it was about 600 to 900 yards to an area that I could rope this bull and tie 'im down and still get back to 'im with a pickup and trailer.

Well, the bull saw me and headed west. Jughead saw the bull and he headed west. The four-year old bronc I was riding saw the bull, and after some minor persuasion, we headed west. (He was a good colt, just a little spooky about big hairy things tearing up brush and making strange noises.)

I finally got the colt running after the bull, and Jughead was working on the bull's head, trying to get 'im slowed up. They went around a big sand hill and some big mesquites, and I noticed that Jughead was barking from another direction.

The colt pulled a one-horse stampede and was running full ahead, wide open, going anywhere.

I quit trying to rein the colt, and just let 'im run. I figured old J.H. had the bull plumb out of the country by this time, and I just concentrated on stayin' ahorseback.

Then I noticed that there was some brush breaking to our left.

Well, me and that colt and the bull came out of the brush at the same time. The bull was running from us, the colt was running from the bull, something was running from Jughead, and I saw my chance to catch the bull.

I hung a spur in the colt's shoulder, pert' near knocked 'im down, and got 'im turned towards the bull. When the colt headed towards the bull, I got two swings on my rope and mailed it.

Now, I have always been afflicted by a dreaded sickness: bad timing.

That colt weighed roughly 1100 pounds, and the bull weighed a little more. The colt was going south and the bull was going west. Jughead had quit barking and I half-headed the bull. To say things came to a halt would be an understatement.

Everything came to a halt but me. When I quit rollin' and got a peek at what was happenin', I noticed a big dust storm.

The colt was just starting to get up and the bull was still down. So I got the shackles out of my leggins and headed for the bull. The bull laid there while I got 'im shackled and his tail tied to the shackles. The colt was just startin' to come back to life.

Well, I headed back to the colt to get my saddle straight and check out my horse. It was at this point that I got my look at the six-point buck deer.

Old J.H. was running a deer!

That deer came out of the brush and was fixin' to

run between me and that colt. The deer was runnin' scared and seeing me didn't bother 'im at all. Bothered the colt, though.

The colt broke to run. He hit the end of the rope and things got tight just about the time the buck hit the rope. The buck got flipped over backwards and J.H. got there just as the buck hit the ground. The buck thought I was the one biting him, and he made a run at me.

While all of this was goin' on, I was screaming at that stupid dog, trying to call 'im off the deer, and the bull was gettin' up, drawin' a bead on me.

I broke to run from the deer and ran smooth over a bull that was a little upset. I came to a halt just in time to get run smooth over by a deer that had a dog hangin' on to a hind leg.

This deer got shed of old J.H. and headed back to the brush. The colt had bucked to the end of the rope and jerked the bull down and stopped himself, and J.H. had taken a lip-lock on the bull, and I was hurtin'.

I finally got the colt calmed down and my rope off the bull. My shirt was just about gone and I couldn't find my cigarettes.

I was so mad at the dog, if I'd had a gun, I would have killed 'im right there.

We got the bull to the sale barn and things leveled out considerable, but old J.H. still pulled some stunts that kept me fuming.

One afternoon I had to go to Artesia and old J.H. managed to bite a city cop. Well, after bailing 'im out of the dog pound, I was ready to kill 'im permanent. I was so mad that I considered giving him to my sister-in-law. But even J.H. didn't deserve that.

As we were leaving Artesia, I heard on the radio that a certain political party was really working on getting all the people registered to vote.

I saw my chance.

I made a U-turn and headed for the political office. Within the hour, I had made J.H. Brummett a registered Democrat!

From then on, all his messin' up made a whole lot more sense.

Curt Brummett's work has appeared in *Team Ropers Times, DeBaca County News, Livestock Weekly,* and *Horse and Rider.* He and his wife Sheila live in Maljamar, New Mexico. They have three daughters; Debbie, Dana and Zane and four grandchildren; Joe, Lonesome, Justa and J. C..

Drawings by Gerald L. Holmes have appeared in the *Hank the Cowdog* series of books, *Beef Magazine, Western Horseman, The Cattleman,* and other places. Gerald has published a cartoon book, *Pickens Country.* He and his wife Carol live in Perryton, Texas, and have two sons.

The typeface used in this book is Palatino; printed by Walsworth Press, Marceline, Missouri.

81

Curt Brummett is now working on a syndicated column entitled *Querecho Flats*. Curt has also become popular as an entertaining speaker for local and national functions. For further information on Curt as a columnist or speaker, please call Laffing Cow Press toll-free at (800) 722-6932.

## Other books by Curt Brummett:

A Snake in the Bathtub

Roping Can Be Hazardous to Your Health

*Included in:* Horsin' Around,
Lawrence Clayton and Kenneth W. Davis, Editors

## Other Authors distributed by Laffing Cow Press:

Ace Reid

Baxter Black

Bob Budd

John Erickson

Jerry Palen

Gwen Petersen

"Doc" Blakely

Roger Pond

Stan Lynde

Lee Pitts

Bob Artley

...and More!

For your FREE Laffing Cow Press catalog
call toll-free (800) 722-6932